COUCHBASE ON KUBERNETES

Autonomously Run and Manage a Complex
Distributed Database on Kubernetes

Anil Kumar

To Couchbase and Kubernetes
Customers and Community

Foreword

We're excited to present this new book to you, our Couchbase customers, users, and readers. We started developing Couchbase Autonomous Operator back in 2017 when we realized how Kubernetes is revolutionizing the way we run infrastructure and enable a host of new technologies and applications. We did not want our customers and users to have to build their solution to run Couchbase Server on Kubernetes, so we designed the "Couchbase Autonomous Operator."

After a few beta releases and helpful feedback from early customers and community users, Couchbase Autonomous Operator 1.0 was released in August 2018. As of this writing in September 2018, there are already dozens of customers testing Couchbase Autonomous Operator in production.

A special thanks to our Couchbase and community colleagues.

We hope you enjoy this book. If you have feedback or suggestions for future topics, please share them on our forums, on Stack Overflow, and of course, send email to anil@couchbase.com.

Anil Kumar
Couchbase Inc.
3250 Olcott Street
Santa Clara, CA 95054
October 2018

Acknowledgments

Writing a book is harder than I thought and more rewarding than I could have ever imagined. None of this would have been possible without my mentor and good friend, Keshav Murthy. Thank you for inspiring me to write this book.

This book is dedicated to my Couchbase engineering group, and the other teams in Couchbase that help define the product, support, and community. Without their hard work and contribution, this book would not exist.

Mike Wiederhold, Engineering Manager – Cloud

Tommie McAfee, Sr. Software Engineer – Cloud

Simon Murray, Sr. Software Engineer – Cloud

Korrigan Clark, Software Engineer in Test

Arunkumar Senthilnathan, Sr. Software Engineer in Test

Ashwin Govindarajulu, Software Engineer in Test

Sindhura Palakodety, Sr. Technical Support Engineer

Matt Carabine, Sr. Technical Support Engineer

Lynn Straus, Sr. Manager, Programs

Eric Schneider, Sr. Technical Writer

Chris Hillery, Sr. Build/Release Engineer

Kenneth Lareau, Sr. Build/Release Engineer

About the Author

Anil Kumar[1] is the Director of Product Management at Couchbase. Anil's career spans more than 15+ years building software products across various domains including enterprise software, mobile services, and voice and video services. As Director of Product Management at Couchbase, he is a hands-on product leader responsible for Couchbase Server, Cloud, and Kubernetes product lines as well as evangelizing the product strategy and vision with customers, partners, developers, and analysts. Prior to joining Couchbase, Anil spent several years working at Microsoft in the Entertainment division and Windows and Windows Live division. Anil holds a master's degree in computer science from Toronto (Canada) and a bachelor's in information technology from Visvesvaraya Technological University (India).

Table of Contents

1. WHAT IS KUBERNETES?

INTRODUCTION TO KUBERNETES – MANAGE AND SCALE YOUR ENTIRE APPLICATION STACK

Kubernetes (originating from the Greek word for "governor," "helmsman," or "captain," and commonly referred to as "K8s"), is an open source container-orchestration technology for automating deployment, scaling, and managing containerized applications. It was developed and open sourced by Google, inspired by a decade of experience deploying scalable, reliable systems in containers, and heavily influenced by Google's Borg[2] system.

Kubernetes open source project is now maintained by the Cloud Native Computing Foundation[3] (CNCF).

Kubernetes is a technology that is built to serve both the needs of internet-scale companies and cloud-native developers of all scales, from a cluster running on a development machine to a datacenter full of sophisticated machines. Kubernetes provides the software necessary to create and deploy reliable, scalable, distributed containerized systems successfully across the entire application stack.

Kubernetes focuses on building a robust orchestration system for running thousands of containers in production. Through automation of processes, Kubernetes can eliminate many of the laborious manual tasks and infrastructure complexity that often fall on DevOps teams to help with the deployment, scaling, and management of containerized applications.

While Kubernetes works mainly with Docker container, it can also work with any container technology that conforms to the Open Container Initiative[4] (OCI) standards for container image formats and runtimes. OCI was established in June 2015 by Docker and other leaders in the container industry.

KUBERNETES ARCHITECTURE

Kubernetes architecture consists of two main components: master node(s) and nodes (see Figure 1.1 next page).

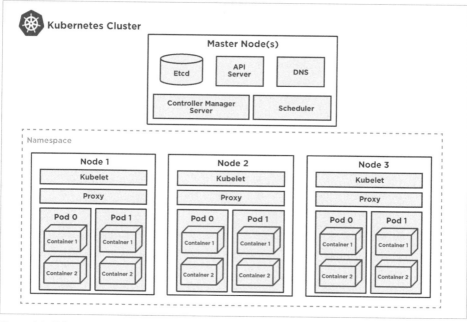

Figure 1.1: Kubernetes architecture

Master Node

The **master node** provides the Kubernetes main cluster management. Master components make global decisions about the cluster and detect and respond to cluster events. Examples of these decisions are scheduling, starting pods, and ensuring that pods are running. The master usually runs on a single node and can have multiple replicas.

Here are the main components of the master node (see Figure 1.2 next page):

1. **API server** – It is the front-end for the Kubernetes control plane, and nearly all the components on the master and worker nodes accomplish their respective tasks by making API calls.

2. **etcd** – etcd is a service whose job is to keep and replicate the current configuration and run the state of the cluster. It is a lightweight, distributed key-value store that was initially developed inside the CoreOS project.

3. **Scheduler and controller manager server** – These processes schedule pods onto target worker nodes. They also make sure that the correct numbers of these pods are running at all times.

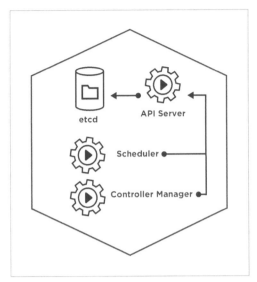

Figure 1.2: Kubernetes master node

Nodes

A **node** is a worker machine in Kubernetes, also referred to as worker nodes. A node might be running on a virtual machine (VM) or physical machine, depending on where the cluster gets deployed. Each node is responsible for maintaining pods (introduced in next section) and providing the Kubernetes runtime environment. Nodes receive tasks from the master and execute those tasks. Examples of tasks are creating new pods, updating network routing, and providing statuses about pods or the node itself.

A node usually runs two critical processes:

1. **Kubelet** – An agent that runs on each node whose job is to respond to commands from the master to create, destroy, and monitor the containers on that host.

2. **Proxy** – This is a simple network proxy that's used to separate the IP address of a target container from the name of the service it provides.

Pods

Pods are the smallest deployable units of computing that can be created and managed in Kubernetes.

Each pod consists of a group of one or more containers, with shared storage, network, and specification for how to run the containers (see Figure 1.3 below).

Containers within a pod share an IP address and port space and can find each other via localhost. They also share volumes, so anything written to disk by one container can be read by another container as long as both containers are in the same pod.

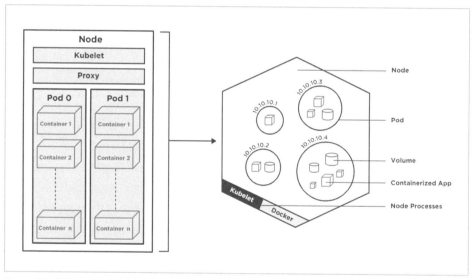

Figure 1.3: Kubernetes node and pod overview

Volumes

In general, there are two types of volume in Kubernetes:

1. Ephemeral volume

2. Persistent volume

Ephemeral Volume

Conceptually, an ephemeral volume is a file directory that is accessible to all of the containers in a pod. The volume source declared in the pod specification[5] determines how the directory gets created, the storage medium used, and the directory's initial contents. A pod specifies what volumes it contains and the path where containers mount the volume.

Ephemeral volume types have the same lifetimes as their enclosing pods. These volumes get created when the pod gets created, and they persist through container restarts. When the pod gets terminated or deleted, its volumes gets deleted along with it (see Figure 1.4 below).

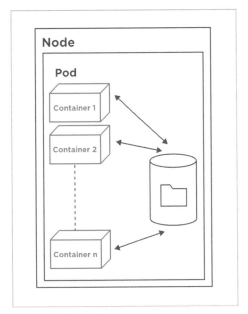

Figure 1.4: Pod ephemeral volume

Persistent Volume

A persistent volume (PV) is a storage location that has a lifetime independent of any pod or container. Independence is very useful in the case of persistent storage solutions where the on-disk representation of a database should survive even if the containers running the database application crash or move to different machines. If the application moves to a different machine, the volume should move with it, and data gets preserved. Separating the data storage out as a persistent volume makes this possible.

PersistentVolume resources can be provisioned dynamically through PersistentVolumeClaims, or a cluster administrator can explicitly create them (see Figure 1.5 below).

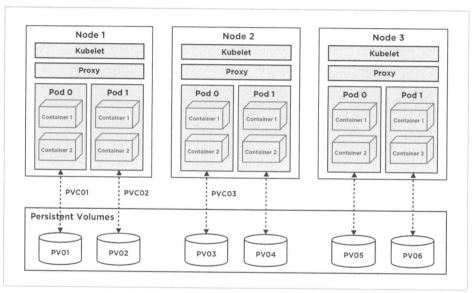

Figure 1.5: Cluster of PersistentVolume attached to pods using PersistentVolumeClaim

GETTING STARTED

As described in Kubernetes documentation, Kubernetes can run on various platforms: from your laptop to VMs on a cloud provider to a rack of bare metal servers. The effort required to set up a cluster varies from running a single command to crafting your customized cluster.

The best way to get started on your local machine is to use Minikube[6] (single-node Kubernetes cluster) or Minishift[7] (single-node OpenShift cluster), which make great development tools.

2. WHY RUN COUCHBASE ON KUBERNETES?

INTRODUCTION – HOW KUBERNETES CONQUERS STATEFUL CLOUD-NATIVE APPLICATIONS

There was a widespread myth that Kubernetes was not ready for stateful applications, and had a surprisingly short life. This myth was driven by a combination of the initial focus on stateless applications within the Kubernetes community and the relatively late addition of support for StatefulSets and persistent storage to the platform.

Further, even after initial support for persistent storage, the kinds of higher-level platform primitives that brought ease of use and flexibility to stateless applications were missing for stateful workloads. However, not only has this shortcoming been addressed, but Kubernetes is fast becoming the preferred platform for **stateful cloud-native applications**.

WHY RUN COUCHBASE ON KUBERNETES?

The proven flexibility and potential Kubernetes has delivered with regard to automating deployment, scalability, and management of containerized applications also applies to containerized, stateful distributed databases such as Couchbase Server.

The main reasons companies consider running Couchbase Server on Kubernetes include:

1. Adopting a hybrid cloud or multi-cloud strategy
2. Moving toward a microservices architecture
3. Managing hundreds of globally distributed multi-cloud deployments

Adopting a Hybrid Cloud or Multi-Cloud Strategy

Many companies are embracing a "cloud-first" strategy, and according to 451 Research, "69% of enterprises will have multi-cloud/hybrid IT environments by 2019."

As enterprises move their business-critical data to the cloud, they are embracing hybrid cloud architecture, which supports an organization's data in both public and private cloud infrastructures.

A hybrid cloud approach provides flexibility regarding the scalability and geo-distribution of data. Increasingly, it is becoming a standard requirement for databases to:

1. Be cloud-agnostics or infrastructure-agnostic and be able to run anywhere – bare metal, VMs, private or public cloud.
2. Provide data migration/replication capability, i.e., freedom to move data to any cloud with fast and efficient data replication technology.

Why does a database need to be cloud-agnostic or infrastructure-agnostic?

With the increased adoption of a hybrid cloud/multi-cloud approach, enterprises are facing a new challenge: cloud vendor lock-in. Enterprises don't want to get "locked-in" to a particular cloud vendor, as their business goals dictate the use of the most price-competitive cloud service, while taking advantage of the speed, capacity, and features offered by a particular cloud provider in a specified geographic region.

Cloud vendor lock-in blocks enterprises from switching between cloud providers since there is little to no industry standardization between these clouds. These challenges are top of mind for enterprises as they move into a multi-cloud environment.

Hence Kubernetes is a "game changer," as it solves the biggest problem facing companies that want to deploy in a cloud-agnostic way.

"A database engineer can now take Couchbase Docker containers, describe it with declarative YAML with all the configuration – environment variables, ports, availability zones, storage systems, and so forth – and then run it on any public or private cloud with zero lock-ins."

Cloud vendor lock-in is no longer a concern because CNCF has created a Certified Kubernetes Conformance Program[8]. Most of the world's leading vendors and cloud computing providers have Certified Kubernetes offerings.

Certified Kubernetes Conformance Program standards include:

1. **Guaranteed portability and interoperability** – users want their workloads to run everywhere.

2. **Timely updates** – to remain certified, vendors need to provide the latest version of Kubernetes yearly or more frequently, so you can be sure that you'll always have access to the latest features the community has been working hard to deliver.

3. **Confirmability** – any end user can confirm that their distribution or platform remains conformant by running the same open source conformance application (Sonobuoy) that was used to certify.

With Kubernetes, enterprises can run a Couchbase cluster on any cloud including Red Hat OpenShift, Google Kubernetes Engine GKE, Amazon Elastic Container Service for Kubernetes EKS, Microsoft's Azure AKS, and Pivotal CloudFoundry Container Runtime. No matter where you deploy the cluster, it runs more or less the same with no glitches or performance issues.

Why does a database need to provide data migration/ replication technology?

Although Kubernetes provides an ability to quickly deploy the same configuration across your private and public multi-clouds, migration of data or data synchronization is still the critical capability that a database needs to provide in order to be genuinely multi-cloud/hybrid cloud.

Couchbase delivers an enterprise-grade solution, cross datacenter replication (XDCR), for data migration or synchronization. Cross datacenter replication is Couchbase's flagship technology for high-performance, (memory-to-memory) network-speed data replication.

XDCR makes it very easy to lift and shift from one cloud to another without requiring any third-party technologies for migrating data. Also, XDCR makes it much easier to distribute data across multi-cloud deployments.

Moving Toward a Microservices Architecture

Microservices have become ubiquitous among enterprise development teams. According to Dimension Research, a Global Microservices Trends survey shows the use of microservices moving at a rapid pace. The vast majority of development teams at large companies (92%) reported an increase in their number of microservices.

The main difference between microservices architecture and monolithic architecture is instead of building an application that includes all of the components in one deployable executable file (monolithic), microservices architecture is a suite of independently deployed and narrowly focused services. By isolating out the monolithic application into smaller parts (services), developers can then enhance, patch, and scale those services as needed without affecting the other ones.

Typically, enterprises moving toward a microservices architecture are adopting containerized platforms using containers and Kubernetes technologies. While organizations take on the journey to microservices architecture by containerization, they often isolate stateless applications running in containers from their stateful application, i.e., database on on-premises or VMs, building new silos in their infrastructure (see Figure 2.1 below).

Hence, enterprises who have adopted microservices architecture for their applications find it very difficult to manage and scale database clusters in a siloed system, making it longer to develop and harder to support their applications.

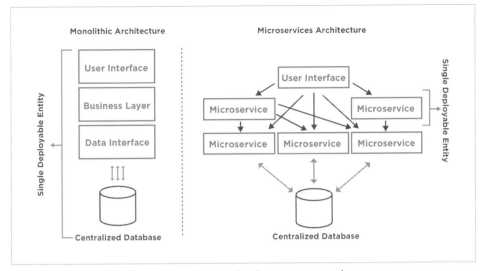

Figure 2.1: Comparison between application development approaches

To solve this database silo challenge and reduce your DevOps workload, run Couchbase as an autonomous, stateful application next to your microservices applications on the same Kubernetes platform.

An important rule for microservices architecture is that each microservice owns its domain data and logic. Just as a full application owns its logic and data, so must each microservice.

There are other advantages to running the data service closer to the microservice such as high performance and low latency. Optionally, for the system of record, data from all the data services can be replicated back to a centralized database (see Figure 2.2 on next page).

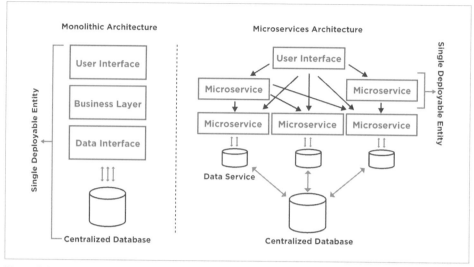

Figure 2.2: Data sovereignty comparison – monolithic database versus microservices

Managing Hundreds of Globally Distributed Multi-Cloud Deployments

Most companies deploy hundreds of database clusters for a variety of reasons, for example, development, test, pre-production, and production setup, which makes sense. Moreover, clusters may have to be deployed in different regions or availability zones for data availability or geo-locality reasons. Also, clusters may need to be deployed across public and private clouds for a hybrid strategy.

As a result, there is a very high operational cost associated with deploying and managing hundreds of clusters across multiple setups, regions, and private and public clouds.

Managing hundreds of clusters is where Kubernetes is once again a "game changer" as it provides software-as-a-service automation capabilities that automate many of the manual processes involved in deploying, scaling, and managing containerized applications.

Deploying and running Couchbase as a containerized stateful application on Kubernetes can reduce up to 90-95% of the operational complexity.

3. KUBERNETES STATEFULSETS AND OPERATOR?

KUBERNETES STATEFULSETS

As mentioned in Kubernetes documentation[9], StatefulSets represent a new set of Kubernetes API objects used to manage stateful applications.

StatefulSets are valuable for applications that require one or more of the following:

- Stable, unique network identifiers
- Stable, persistent storage
- Ordered, graceful deployment and scaling
- Ordered, graceful deletion and termination
- Ordered, automated rolling updates

In the above list, stable is synonymous with persistence across pod (re)scheduling. If an application doesn't require any stable identifiers or ordered deployment, deletion, or scaling you should deploy your application with a controller that provides a set of stateless replicas. Controllers such as deployment[10] or replicaSet[11] may be better suited to your stateless needs.

The state information and other resilient data for any given StatefulSet pod get maintained in persistent volumes[12] associated with the StatefulSet (see Figure 3.1 next page).

The example below demonstrates the components of a StatefulSet:

- A "headless" service is used to control the network domain
- The StatefulSets, pods with unique, persistent identities, and stable hostnames that Kubernetes Engine maintains regardless of where they are scheduled
- The PersistentVolumeClaim PVC provides stable storage using PersistentVolumes provisioned by a PersistentVolume provisioner

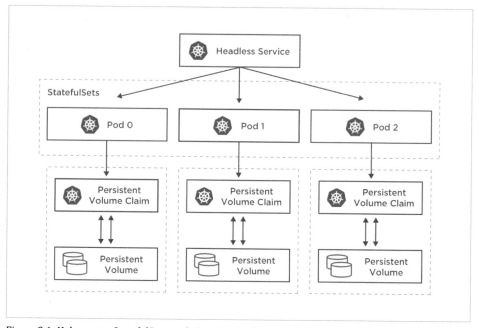

Figure 3.1: Kubernetes StatefulSets with PersistentVolumeClaim and persistent volume

Here is the comparison of a StatefulSet pod versus a stateless pod.

StatefulSet Pod	Stateless Pod
File Server – file server needs to maintain persistent storage across restarts	Ephemeral data, nothing is persisted to storage or disk
Logs – to collect support information and log analysis	Does not care about previous state

Figure 3.1: StatefulSets versus stateless

KUBERNETES OPERATOR

A Kubernetes Operator is an application-specific controller[13] that extends the Kubernetes API to create, configure, and manage instances of complex stateful applications on behalf of a Kubernetes user. It builds upon the necessary Kubernetes resource and controller concepts but includes the domain or application-specific knowledge to automate everyday tasks.

Operators were first introduced by CoreOS as a class of software that operates other software, putting operational knowledge collected by humans into the software. Read more in the original blog post, Introducing Operators: Putting Operational Knowledge into Software.[14]

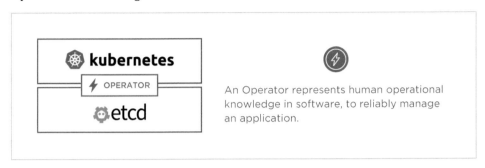

An Operator represents human operational knowledge in software, to reliably manage an application.

Operators build upon two central Kubernetes concepts: resources and controllers. As an example, the built-in ReplicaSet resource lets users set a desired number of pods to run, and controllers inside Kubernetes ensure the desired state set in the ReplicaSet resource remains true by creating or removing running pods. There are many fundamental controllers and resources in Kubernetes that work in this manner, including Services, Deployments, and DaemonSets.

Here's a list of excellent operators:

https://github.com/operator-framework/awesome-operators

STATEFULSETS VERSUS OPERATOR

Limitations of StatefulSets

Limitation #1

StatefulSets are great for specific use cases where each pod in the StatefulSet doesn't need to interact with other pods in the same StatefulSet. For example, file servers need to maintain the same persistent storage across restarts and can quickly be deployed and restarted without the execution of custom logic. As long as other applications in the cluster discover it, then it can quickly be run with a StatefulSet.

Whereas for running complex distributed databases, such as Couchbase that requires different custom logic to properly deploy, scale, and maintain a cluster, StatefulSets focus on creating and managing pods, not on managing the complicated software running on them.

Limitation #2

When a pod gets terminated or deleted with a StatefulSet, Kubernetes tries to recreate the pod on the same node it was running on previously. Kubernetes doesn't want a pod to be immediately restarted on another node in order to reduce a possible split-brain scenario, and multiple instances of the same pod can lead to data corruption. Recreating the pod on the same node is the default nature of a StatefulSet because Kubernetes assumes that the applications running in a StatefulSet require a stable network identity and stable storage.

If a node/host becomes unreachable because it's down for scheduled maintenance or becomes partitioned from the network, Kubernetes then schedules a pod to be created on another node, and the secondary disk gets moved to that node. Unfortunately, the timeframe for new pod creation can result in data unavailability for the application when a pod doesn't get restarted on another node.

Need for Operator: Stateless Is Easy, Stateful Is Hard

With Kubernetes, it is relatively easy to manage and scale web apps, mobile backends, and API services right out of the box. Why? Because these applications are generally stateless, so the basic Kubernetes APIs, like Deployments, can scale and recover from failures without additional knowledge.

A more significant challenge is managing stateful applications, like databases such as Couchbase Server. These systems require application domain knowledge to correctly scale, upgrade, and reconfigure while protecting against data loss or unavailability. We want this application-specific operational knowledge encoded into software that leverages the powerful Kubernetes abstractions to run and manage the application correctly.

An Operator is software that encodes this domain knowledge and extends the Kubernetes API through the third-party resources[15] mechanism, enabling users to create, configure, and manage applications. Like Kubernetes's built-in resources, an Operator doesn't just manage a single instance of the application, but multiple instances across the cluster.

For example, by deploying a unique custom Couchbase controller, Kubernetes gets Couchbase-specific knowledge, and as each Couchbase pod gets deployed, it can adequately configure and join it with the other Couchbase pods in the cluster. It's also important to keep in mind that provisioning a cluster is just one place where having a custom controller helps to automate tasks – node failure, ad hoc scaling, and many other management tasks also require Couchbase-specific knowledge within Kubernetes in order to be properly automated.

4. INTRODUCING COUCHBASE AUTONOMOUS OPERATOR FOR KUBERNETES

INTRODUCTION

The **Couchbase Autonomous Operator** provides native integration of Couchbase Server with Open Source Kubernetes and Red Hat OpenShift. It enables you to automate the management of everyday Couchbase tasks such as the configuration, creation, scaling, and recovery of Couchbase clusters. By reducing the complexity of running a Couchbase cluster, it lets you focus on the desired configuration and not worry about the details of manual deployment and lifecycle management.

Why It Is Called "Autonomous"

In general, autonomous software means self-healing and self-managing intelligent systems.

The goal of the Autonomous Operator is to fully self-manage one or more Couchbase deployments so that you don't need to worry about the operational complexities of running Couchbase. Not only does the Autonomous Operator automatically administer your Couchbase cluster, it also self-heals and self-manages the cluster according to Couchbase best practices.

How Autonomous Operator Works

The Autonomous Operator works by extending the Kubernetes API through the use of a CustomResourceDefinition[16] (CRD). This allows us to create a custom native resource in Kubernetes that is similar to a StatefulSet or a Deployment, but in this case, is designed specifically for managing a Couchbase deployment.

What are Kubernetes built-in resources?

Here is a high-level overview of the basic types of resources provided by the Kubernetes API and their primary functions.

- **Workloads** are objects used to manage and run containers on the cluster
- **Discovery & LB** resources are objects used to "stitch" workloads together into an externally accessible, load-balanced service
- **Config & Storage** resources are objects used to inject initialization data into applications and to persist data that is external to the container

- **Cluster** resources are objects used to define how the cluster itself is configured; these are typically used solely by cluster operators

- **Metadata** resources are objects used to configure the behavior of other resources within the cluster, such as HorizontalPodAutoscaler for scaling workloads

Kubernetes provides APIs to read and write Kubernetes built-in resource objects via a Kubernetes API endpoint. Autonomous Operator uses those APIs to manage resources for multiple instances across an entire Kubernetes cluster.

Autonomous Operator simulates the behavior of a DevOps DBA by observing the current state of the Couchbase cluster, finding differences between the desired state and the current state of the cluster, and then taking steps to alter the cluster so that it matches the desired state. The steps are all achieved through the use of the Kubernetes and Couchbase APIs.

For example, let's say you want to scale your Couchbase cluster from three instances to five instances to handle more workload. Autonomous Operator would first look at the current state of the cluster, and using the Kubernetes API, it will check how many instances are currently in the cluster, then check the number of instances desired against the current state of the cluster, and see that two more instances need to get added. The Autonomous Operator would then use the Kubernetes API to provision a fourth and fifth instance, and use the Couchbase API to add the new instances to the Couchbase cluster and rebalance them in.

To illustrate this behavior, let's see how Autonomous Operator works when new instances are added to a cluster (see Figure 4.1 next page).

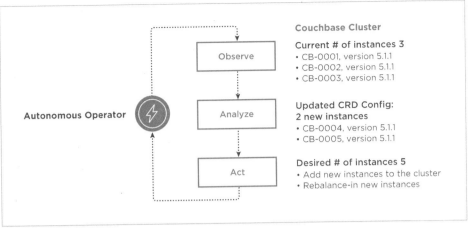

Figure 4.1: Autonomous Operator – observe, analyze, and act

COUCHBASE AUTONOMOUS OPERATOR ARCHITECTURE

Autonomous Operator architecture consists of the following components (see Figure 4.2 next page):

1. Server pods

2. Services

3. Volumes

When a Couchbase cluster gets deployed, additional Kubernetes resources such as server pods, services, and volumes are created by the Autonomous Operator to facilitate its deployment. All resources originating from the Autonomous Operator get labeled to make it easy to list and describe the resources belonging to a specific cluster.

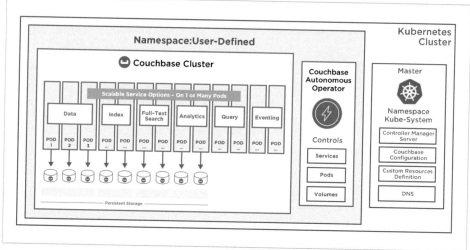

Figure 4.2: Couchbase Autonomous Operator architecture

Server Pods

Autonomous Operator creates Couchbase pods that get labeled by cluster and according to Couchbase service, which makes it possible to pinpoint the pods providing a specific Couchbase service for a specific cluster.

Services

Services are created to facilitate both pod-to-pod communication and connections from external clients to the internal cluster. The former is established using a Kubernetes headless service, and the latter via the NodePort service. You can read more about Kubernetes services here.[17]

Volumes

As described earlier, Autonomous Operator supports both types of Kubernetes volumes – ephemeral and persistent volumes.

We are looking forward to Kubernetes support for Persistent Local Storage as it is the best fit for running databases, but in the meantime, we use ephemeral storage by default unless persistent volume is configured.

GETTING STARTED WITH AUTONOMOUS OPERATOR

To install the Autonomous Operator, all you need is a running Kubernetes or OpenShift cluster.

If you don't have access to a Kubernetes cluster, but still want to use the Autonomous Operator for development, Minikube (single-node Kubernetes cluster) and Minishift (single-node OpenShift cluster) make great alternatives. Both of these products are much easier to install and deploy when compared to setting up and running an actual Kubernetes or OpenShift cluster.

You can read about the prerequisites[18] and guidelines and best practices[19] for Autonomous Operator which makes deploying Couchbase Server incredibly simple.

Once you have a Kubernetes or OpenShift cluster, you can then deploy Autonomous Operator. The following links provide the complete instructions for deploying Autonomous Operator on Open Source Kubernetes and Red Hat OpenShift.

You can download the Autonomous Operator package[20] from Couchbase and unpack it on the same computer where you usually run the Kubernetes command-line tool, *kubectl*.

The Autonomous Operator package contains YAML configuration files and command-line tools that you can use to install the Autonomous Operator and Couchbase clusters.

The Autonomous Operator Configuration

The Autonomous Operator configuration mainly specifies deployment kind, namespace, Docker image, service account, and replica count (see Figure 4.3 next page).

When loaded into Kubernetes, it downloads the couchbase/operator[21] Docker image from DockerHub, creates the CouchbaseCluster custom resource definition (CRD), and starts listening for CouchbaseCluster events.

```
apiVersion: extensions/v1beta1
kind: Deployment
metadata:
  name: couchbase-operator
spec:
  replicas: 1
  selector:
    matchLabels:
      app: couchbase-operator
  template:
    metadata:
      labels:
        app: couchbase-operator
    spec:
      containers:
        - name: couchbase-operator
          image: couchbase/operator:1.0.0
          command:
            - couchbase-operator
          args:
            - -create-crd
          env:
            - name: MY_POD_NAMESPACE
              valueFrom:
                fieldRef:
                  fieldPath: metadata.namespace
            - name: MY_POD_NAME
              valueFrom:
                fieldRef:
                  fieldPath: metadata.name
          ports:
            - name: readiness-port
              containerPort: 8080
          readinessProbe:
            httpGet:
              path: /readyz
              port: readiness-port
            initialDelaySeconds: 3
            periodSeconds: 3
            failureThreshold: 19
      serviceAccountName: couchbase-operator
```

Figure 4.3: Couchbase Autonomous Operator configuration

Changing the Namespace

By default, the Autonomous Operator gets deployed in *default* namespace unless you change the *metadata.namespace* field. By design, the Autonomous Operator manages Couchbase clusters deployed in the namespace that are within the same namespace. There has been some discussion in the Kubernetes community to allow Operators to manage deployments across namespaces, but it's not yet fully implemented and available in Kubernetes.

Changing the Autonomous Operator Container Image

If you're not pulling the image from the official Couchbase Docker repository, you change the *spec.spec.containers[0].image* field to update the Autonomous Operator container image location.

If you're running the Autonomous Operator in Red Hat OpenShift, then the container images get pulled from *registry.connect.redhat.com/couchbase/ operator:1.0.0-1*. Before creating the Autonomous Operator, you must first create a personal secret by presenting a valid username and password as follows:

```
$ oc create secret docker-registry rh-catalog --docker-
server=registry.connect.redhat.com --docker-username=<CUSTOMER
USERNAME> --docker-password=<CUSTOMER PASSWORD> --docker-
email=<VALID REDHAT EMAIL>
```

For example:

```
$ oc create secret docker-registry rh-catalog --docker-
server=registry.connect.redhat.com --docker-username=redcouch
--docker-password=openshift --docker-email=redcouchredhat@gmail.com
```

Then we created a secret to pull it into the registry:

```
$ oc secrets add serviceaccount/couchbase-operator secrets/rh-catalog
--for=pull
$ oc secrets add serviceaccount/default secrets/rh-catalog --for=pull
```

Changing the Name

By default, the name of the deployment gets created for the Autonomous Operator and is called *couchbase-operator*. If you need to change it for some reason, ensure that you change the *metadata.name, spec.template.metadata.labels.name*, and *spec.spec.containers[0].name* fields. These fields must all have the same value.

It is recommended that you use the *couchbase-operator name* since it is used in all of the examples and tutorials in our documentation.[22]

Changing the Service Account

You can update the *spec.spec. serviceAccountName* for your environment in the sample configuration it uses for *couchbase-operator*. Note that this field only takes effect if your Kubernetes environment has been RBAC enabled.

Changing the Replica Count

Usually, deployments are used to create multiple instances of a pod to provide redundancy. However, when deploying the Autonomous Operator, you should always set replicas to 1 because the Autonomous Operator pod uses leader election to ensure that only one Kubernetes Operator is running in a specific namespace. If you start more than one Autonomous Operator pod in the same namespace, only the first one gets created successfully. The Autonomous Operator uses a deployment controller so that if the Autonomous Operator pod dies, a new Autonomous Operator pod gets created and picks up from where the old one left off.

Create the Autonomous Operator

You can now create and start the Autonomous Operator by running one single command:

```
kubectl create -f operator.yaml
```

After you run the "kubectl create" command, it generally takes less than a minute for Kubernetes to deploy the Autonomous Operator and for the Autonomous Operator to be ready to run.

Prerequisites for Deploying a Couchbase Cluster

Before deploying a Couchbase cluster with the Autonomous Operator, ensure that you have done the following:

- Reviewed the prerequisites
- Deployed the Autonomous Operator, and verified it is up and running
- Downloaded the Autonomous Operator package from Couchbase and installed *cbopctl*

Note: *cbopctl* is a command-line tool similar to *kubectl* or *oc*, except that it performs an extra check on the CouchbaseCluster configuration being sent to Kubernetes to ensure that it is valid.

cbopctl is the recommended way to install Couchbase Server with Autonomous Operator 1.0 since Kubernetes 1.9 and 1.10 does not ship CRD validation yet. As of this writing CRD validation is beta in Kubernetes 1.11.

The Autonomous Operator package also contains YAML configuration files that will help you set up a Couchbase cluster.

CouchbaseCluster Configuration

Here is a sample configuration file for the CouchbaseCluster (see Figure 4.4 next page). The top-level parameters for a CouchbaseCluster configuration include – *apiversion*, *kind*, *metadata*, and *spec*.

```
apiVersion: couchbase.com/v1
kind: CouchbaseCluster
metadata:
  name: cb-example
spec:
  baseImage: couchbase/server
  version: enterprise-5.5.1
  authSecret: cb-example-auth
  exposeAdminConsole: true
  adminConsoleServices:
    - data
  cluster:
    dataServiceMemoryQuota: 256
    indexServiceMemoryQuota: 256
    searchServiceMemoryQuota: 256
    eventingServiceMemoryQuota: 256
    analyticsServiceMemoryQuota: 1024
    indexStorageSetting: memory_optimized
    autoFailoverTimeout: 120
    autoFailoverMaxCount: 3
    autoFailoverOnDataDiskIssues: true
    autoFailoverOnDataDiskIssuesTimePeriod: 120
    autoFailoverServerGroup: false
  buckets:
    - name: default
      type: couchbase
      memoryQuota: 128
      replicas: 1
      ioPriority: high
      evictionPolicy: fullEviction
      conflictResolution: seqno
      enableFlush: true
      enableIndexReplica: false
  servers:
    - size: 3
      name: all_services
      services:
        - data
        - index
        - query
        - search
        - eventing
        - analytics
```

Figure 4.4: CouchbaseCluster configuration

apiVersion

The *apiVersion* field specifies the Kubernetes API version we're using to create the Autonomous Operator object. You can update the API version whenever new features are added. For any given release, the API versions that are supported by the Autonomous Operator will be specified in the documentation. It is recommended that you upgrade to the latest API version whenever possible.

Field rules: The *apiVersion* field is required and must be set to a valid API version. The value of this field cannot be changed after the cluster is created.

kind

The *kind* field specifies that the Kubernetes configuration will use the custom Couchbase controller to manage the cluster.

Field rules: The *kind* field is required and must always be set to CouchbaseCluster. The value of this field cannot be changed after the cluster is created.

metadata

The *metadata* field allows setting a name for the Couchbase cluster and a namespace that the cluster should be deployed in.

Field rules: A name is highly recommended, but not required. If values are not set in the metadata field, then defaults will be enabled. The value of name will be autogenerated and the value of namespace will be set to default. The value of these fields cannot be changed after the cluster is created.

spec

This section describes the top-level parameters related to a Couchbase cluster deployment.

baseImage

The *baseImage* field specifies the image that should be used.

Field rules: The *baseImage* field is required and should be set to *couchbase/server* unless you want Kubernetes to pull the Couchbase Server Docker container from a different location. The value of this field cannot be changed after the cluster is created.

version

The *version* field specifies the version number of Couchbase Server to install. This should match an available version number in the Couchbase Docker repository. It may never be changed to a lower version number than the version that is currently running.

Field rules: The *version* field is required and should be set to the version of Couchbase Server that should be used to build the cluster. The value of this field cannot be changed after the cluster is created.

paused

The *paused* field specifies whether or not the Autonomous Operator is currently managing the cluster. This parameter should generally be set to *true* but may be set to *false* if you decide to make manual changes to the cluster.

By disabling the Autonomous Operator, you can change the cluster configuration without having to worry about the Autonomous Operator reverting the changes. However, before re-enabling the Autonomous Operator, ensure that the Kubernetes configuration matches the cluster configuration.

Field rules: The *paused* field is not required and defaults to *false* if not specified.

antiAffinity

The *antiAffinity* field specifies whether or not two pods in the cluster can be deployed on the same Kubernetes node. In a production setting this parameter should always be set to *true* in order to reduce the chance of data loss in case a host Kubernetes node crashes.

Field rules: The *antiAffinity* field is not required and defaults to *false* if not specified. The value of this field cannot be changed after the cluster is created.

tls

The *tls* field is optional and controls whether the Autonomous Operator uses TLS for communication with the cluster. It also sets the TLS certificates that are used by Couchbase clients and XDCR. Refer to the TLS documentation[23] for more information.

authSecret

The *authSecret* field specifies the name of a Kubernetes secret that should be used as the user name and password of the Couchbase superuser.

Field rules: The *authSecret* field is required and should reference the name of a Kubernetes secret[24] that already exists. The value of this field cannot be changed after the cluster is created.

exposeAdminConsole

The *exposeAdminConsole* field specifies whether or not the Couchbase Server Web Console should be exposed externally. Exposing the web console is done using a NodePort service, and the port for the service can be found in the describe output when describing this cluster. This parameter may be changed while the cluster is running, and the Autonomous Operator will create/destroy the NodePort service as appropriate.

Field rules: The *exposeAdminConsole* field is not required and defaults to *false* if not specified. If set to *true* the specification must also have the adminConsoleServices property defined.

adminConsoleServices

When the Couchbase Server Web Console is exposed with the *exposeAdminConsole* property, by default, opening a browser session to the Web Console will be automatically load balanced across all pods in the cluster to provide high availability. However, the Web Console will display different features based on the services that are running on the particular pod that it's connected to.

This property allows the UI service to be constrained to pods running one or more specific services. The services that you specify are subtractive in nature – they will only identify pods running all of those services – so care must be used. For example, if the cluster is deployed with multi-dimensional scaling, the data service on one set of pods and the analytics service on another mutually exclusive set, then specifying data and analytics as your Web Console services list would result in the Web Console not being accessible – no pods match all the constraints (i.e., no pods are running both the data and analytics services).

If you require access to a specific pod running a specific service, this can also be achieved by using the admin option of the *exposedFeatures* property. This will allow access via a NodePort. You must connect directly to the IP address of the node that the pod is running on. The assigned NodePort is available via the cluster status structure returned by *kubectl describe*, or via the output of *kubectl get services*. Refer to the services documentation for more information.

Field rules: The *adminConsoleServices* list is not required and defaults to an empty list. Valid item names are data, index, query, search, eventing, and analytics, and must be unique. An empty list means that any node in the cluster may be chosen when connecting to the Couchbase Server Web Console.

exposedFeatures

The *exposedFeatures* field specifies a list of per-pod features to expose on the cluster network (as opposed to the pod network). These define sets of ports which are required to support the specified features. The supported values are as follows:

- *admin* – Exposes the admin API and UI
- *xdcr* – Exposes the ports necessary to support XDCR via L3 connectivity at the cluster network layer
- *client* – Exposes all client services, which include data, views, query, full-text search, and analytics

Field rules: The *exposedFeatures* list is optional; no feature sets are exposed to the cluster network if unset.

softwareUpdateNotifications

The *softwareUpdateNotifications* field specifies whether or not software update notifications are displayed in the Couchbase UI. This provides a visual indication as to whether a software update is available and should be applied in order to increase functionality or fix defects.

Field rules: The *softwareUpdateNotifications* field is optional and defaults to *false* if not specified. This setting can be modified at any point in the cluster lifecycle.

serverGroups

Setting the field enables automatic management of Couchbase server groups. The end user is responsible for adding labels to their Kubernetes nodes which will be used to evenly distribute nodes across server groups, so the cluster is tolerant to the loss of an entire data *serverGroups* center (or any other desired failure domain). Nodes are labeled with a key of *failure-domain.beta.kubernetes.io/zone* and an arbitrary name string. Multiple nodes may have the same server group to allow multiple pods to be scheduled there regardless of antiAffinity settings. An example of applying the label is as follows:

```
kubectl label nodes ip-172-22-22-22 failure-
domain.beta.kubernetes.io/zone=us-east-1a
```

As the list of server groups to use is explicit, the end user has flexibility in controlling exactly where pods will be scheduled (e.g., one cluster may reside in one set of server groups, and another cluster in another set of server groups).

At present, the scheduling simply stripes pods across the server groups; each new pod is run in a server group with the fewest existing cluster members. This is performed on a per-server configuration basis to ensure individual classes of servers are equally distributed for high availability. For each class of server configuration, you may choose to override the set of server groups to schedule across. For additional information, see the documentation under the *spec. servers.serverGroups* configuration key.

The server group feature does not support service redistribution at this time, so scaling the set of server groups will not result in any pods being "moved" to make best use of the new topology or evacuated from a removed server group.

Field rules: The *serverGroups* field is optional. If pods will be scheduled across the specified set of server groups, the server groups must be set at cluster creation time, and, at this time, should be assumed to be immutable.

securityContext

The *securityContext* field is a Kubernetes PodSecurityContext object which is attached to all pods that are created by the Autonomous Operator. If unspecified, this will default to the *couchbase* user, mount attached volumes as that user, and ensure that the containers are running as non-root. You may override the default behavior if using a custom container image or for testing purposes.

Field rules: The *securityContext* field is optional. If set, this will be attached to all new pods that are created by the Autonomous Operator. This field should not be modified during the cluster lifecycle.

disableBucketManagement

The *disableBucketManagement* field specifies whether to ignore the bucket configuration. When *disableBucketManagement* is set to *false* (the default), the Autonomous Operator will have sole control over creating the buckets that are specified in the configuration (and deleting the buckets that are not).

If set to *true*, the creation and deletion of buckets must be done manually using the Couchbase Server Web Console, CLI, REST API, or SDK. Even if buckets are specified in the configuration, as long as *disableBucketManagement* is set to *false*, the Autonomous Operator will not create or delete any buckets.

Field rules: The *disableBucketManagement* field is optional and defaults to *false*.

spec.cluster

This section describes the various Couchbase cluster settings. This section is not meant to encompass every setting that is configurable on Couchbase. Cluster settings not mentioned here can be managed manually.

dataServiceMemoryQuota

The *dataServiceMemoryQuota* field is the amount of memory to assign to the data service if it is present on a specific Couchbase node. The amount of memory is defined in megabytes (MB).

Field rules: The *dataServiceMemoryQuota* field is required and must be set to be greater than or equal to 256. Keep in mind that the sum of all memory quotas must be no more than 80% of a pod's available memory.

indexServiceMemoryQuota

The *indexServiceMemoryQuota* field is the amount of memory to assign to the index service if it is present on a specific Couchbase node. The amount of memory is defined in megabytes (MB).

Field rules: The *indexServiceMemoryQuota* field is required and must be set to be greater than or equal to 256. Keep in mind that the sum of all memory quotas must be no more than 80% of a pod's available memory.

searchServiceMemoryQuota

The *searchServiceMemoryQuota* field is the amount of memory to assign to the search service if it is present on a specific Couchbase node. The amount of memory is defined in megabytes (MB). This parameter defaults to 256MB if it is not set.

Field rules: The *searchServiceMemoryQuota* field is required and must be set to be greater than or equal to 256. Keep in mind that the sum of all memory quotas must be no more than 80% of a pod's available memory.

eventingServiceMemoryQuota

The *eventingSearchMemoryQuota* field is the amount of memory to assign to the eventing service if it is present on a specific Couchbase node. The amount of memory is defined in megabytes (MB). This parameter defaults to 256MB if it is not set.

Field rules: The *eventingServiceMemoryQuota* field is required and must be set to be greater than or equal to 256. Keep in mind that the sum of all memory quotas must be no more than 80% of a pod's available memory.

analyticsServiceMemoryQuota

The *analyticsServiceMemoryQuota* field is the amount of memory to assign to the search service if it is present on a specific Couchbase node. The amount of memory is defined in megabytes (MB). This parameter defaults to 1,024MB if it is not set.

Field rules: The *analyticsServiceMemoryQuota* field is required and must be set to be greater than or equal to 1,024. Keep in mind that the sum of all memory quotas must be no more than 80% of a pod's available memory.

indexStorageSetting

The *indexStorageSetting* field specifies the backend storage type to use for the index service. If the cluster already contains a Couchbase Server instance running the index service, then this parameter cannot be changed until all Couchbase instances running the index service are removed.

Field rules: The *indexStorageSetting* is required and must be set to either plasma or memory-optimized. The value of this field can only be changed if there are no index nodes in the cluster.

autoFailoverTimeout

The *autoFailoverTimeout* field specifies the auto-failover timeout in seconds. The Autonomous Operator relies on the CouchbaseCluster to auto-failover nodes before removing them, so setting this field to an appropriate value is important.

Field rules: The *autoFailoverTimeout* is required and must be in the range of 5-3,600sec.

autoFailoverMaxCount

The *autoFailoverMaxCount* field specifies the maximum number of failover events that can be tolerated before manual intervention is required. If a bucket has two replicas, it can tolerate two pods failing over. This also applies to entire server groups.

Field rules: The *autoFailoverMaxCount* is required and must be in the range of 1-3.

autoFailoverOnDataDiskIssues

The *autoFailoverOnDataDiskIssues* field specifies whether a node will automatically failover on data disk issues.

Field rules: The *autoFailoverOnDataDiskIssues* is required and must be *true* or *false*.

autoFailoverOnDataDiskIssuesTimePeriod

The *autoFailoverOnDataDiskIssuesTimePeriod* field specifies the time period to wait before automatically failing over a node experiencing data disk issues. This field's units are in seconds.

Field rules: The *autoFailoverOnDataDiskIssuesTimePeriod* is only required if *autoFailoverOnDataDiskIssues* is also set to *true*, and must be in the range of 5-3,600sec.

autoFailoverServerGroup

The *autoFailoverServerGroup* field specifies whether the cluster will automatically failover an entire server group.

Field rules: The *autoFailoverServerGroup* is optional, defaulting to *false*.

spec.buckets

This section describes one or more buckets that must be created in the cluster.

name

The *name* field specifies the name of the bucket. This parameter is required when specifying a bucket.

Field rules: The *name* is required and must be a string using characters and numbers. The value of this field cannot be changed after the bucket is created.

type

The *type* field specifies the type of bucket to create. This parameter can be set to *couchbase*, *ephemeral*, or *memcached*. If the type is not specified, it defaults to *couchbase*.

Field rules: The *type* is required and must be set to *couchbase, ephemeral,* or *memcached.* The value of this field cannot be changed after the bucket is created.

memoryQuota

The *memoryQuota* field specifies the amount of memory to allocate to this bucket in megabytes (MB). If the quota is not specified, it defaults to 100.

Field rules: The *memoryQuota* is required and must be set to greater than or equal to 100.

replicas

The *replicas* field specifies the number of replicas that should be created for this bucket. This value may be set between 0 and 3 inclusive. If the number is not set, it defaults to 1. Note that this parameter has no effect for the memcached bucket type.

Field rules: The *replicas* field is required for buckets with type *couchbase* and *ephemeral* and must be set between 0 and 3. *Memcached* buckets will ignore values in this field. Changing the value of this field will cause a rebalance to occur.

ioPriority

The *ioPriority* field sets the IO priority of background threads for this bucket. This option is valid for *couchbase* and *ephemeral* buckets only. *Memcached* buckets will ignore values in this field.

Field rules: The *ioPriority* is required for buckets with type *couchbase* and *ephemeral* and must be set to either *high* or *low. Memcached* buckets will ignore values in this field. Changing the value of this field will cause downtime while the bucket is restarted.

evictionPolicy

The *evictionPolicy* field sets the memory-cache eviction policy for this bucket. This option is valid for *couchbase* and *ephemeral* buckets only.

Couchbase buckets support either *valueOnly* or *fullEviction*. Specifying the *valueOnly* policy means that each key stored in this bucket must be kept in memory. This is the default policy; using this policy improves the performance of key-value operations but limits the maximum size of the bucket. Specifying the *fullEviction* policy means that the performance is impacted for key-value operations, but the maximum size of the bucket is unbounded.

Ephemeral buckets support either *noEviction* or *nruEviction*. Specifying *noEviction* means that the bucket will not evict items from the cache if the cache is full. This type of eviction policy should be used for in-memory database use cases.

Specifying *nruEviction* means that items not recently used will be evicted from memory when all the memory in the bucket is used. This type of eviction policy should be used for caching use cases.

Field rules: The *evictionPolicy* is required for buckets with type *couchbase* and *ephemeral*. *Memcached* buckets will ignore values in this field. Changing the value of this field will cause downtime while the bucket is restarted.

conflictResolution

The *conflictResolution* field specifies the bucket's conflict resolution mechanism which is to be used if a conflict occurs during cross datacenter replication (XDCR). There are two supported mechanisms: sequence-based and timestamp-based.

The sequence-based conflict resolution mechanism selects the document that has been updated the greatest number of times since the last sync. For example, if one cluster has updated a document twice since the last sync, and the other cluster has updated the document three times, the document updated three times is selected regardless of the specific times at which these updates took place.

The timestamp-based conflict resolution mechanism selects the document with the most recent timestamp. This is only supported when all of the clocks on all of the nodes are fully synchronized.

Field rules: The *conflictResolution* field is required for buckets with type *couchbase* and *ephemeral* and can be set to either *seqno* or *lww*. *Memcached* buckets will ignore values in this field. The value of this field cannot be changed after the bucket has been created.

enableFlush

The *enableFlush* field specifies whether or not to enable the flush command on this bucket. This parameter defaults to *false* if it is not specified. This parameter only affects *couchbase* and *ephemeral* buckets.

Field rules: The *enableFlush* field can be set to either *true* or *false*. If this parameter is not specified, it defaults to *false*.

enableIndexReplica

The *enableIndexReplica* field specifies whether or not to enable view index replicas for this bucket. This parameter defaults to *false* if it is not specified. This parameter only affects *couchbase* buckets.

Field rules: The *enableIndexReplica* field is required for buckets with type *couchbase* and can be set to either *true* or *false*. *Memcached* and *ephemeral* buckets will ignore values in this field.

spec.servers

In the *spec.servers* field, you must specify at least one – but possibly multiple – node specifications. A node specification is used to allow multi-dimensional scaling[25] of a Couchbase cluster with Kubernetes.

Specification rules: The server's portion of the specification is required and must always contain at least one server definition. There must also be at least one definition that contains the data service.

size

The *size* field specifies the number of nodes of this type that should be in the cluster. This allows the user to scale up different parts of the cluster as necessary. If this parameter is changed at runtime, the Autonomous Operator will automatically scale the cluster.[26]

Field rules: The *size* is required and can be set to greater than or equal to 1.

name

The *name* field specifies a name for this group of servers.

Field rules: The *name* field is required and must be unique in comparison to the name field of other server definitions. The value of this field cannot be changed after a server has been defined.

services

The *services* field specifies a list of services that should be run on nodes of this type. Users can specify data, index, query, search, eventing, and analytics in the list. At least one service must be specified, and all clusters must contain at least one node specification that includes the data service.

Field rules: The *services* list is required and must contain at least one service. Valid values for services are data, index, query, search, eventing, and analytics. The values of this list cannot be changed after a server has been defined.

serverGroups

The *serverGroups* field controls the set of server groups to schedule pods in. Functionality is identical to that defined in the top-level specification but overrides it and allows the end user to specify exactly where pods of individual server/service configuration are scheduled. See serverGroups[27] documentation for more details.

spec.servers.pod

The pod policy defines settings that apply to all pods deployed with this node configuration. A pod always contains a single running instance of Couchbase Server.

couchbaseEnv

The *couchbaseEnv* field specifies the environment variables (as key-value pairs) that should be set when the pod is started. This section is optional.

Field rules: The value of *couchbaseEnv* field cannot be changed after a server has been defined.

resources

- *limits* – This field lets you reserve resources on a specific node. It defines the maximum amount of CPU, memory, and storage the pods created in this node specification will reserve.
- *requests* – This field lets you reserve resources on a specific node. The requests section defines the minimum amount of CPU, memory, and storage the pods created in this node specification will reserve.

labels

Labels are key-value pairs that are attached to objects in Kubernetes. They are intended to specify identifying attributes of objects that are meaningful to the user and do not directly imply semantics to the core system. Labels can be used to organize and select subsets of objects. They do not need to be unique across multiple objects. This section is optional.

Labels added in this section will apply to all pods added in this cluster. Note that by default we add the following labels to each pod, which should not be overridden.

```
app:couchbase
couchbase_cluster:<metadata:name>
```

In the sample configuration file referenced in this topic, the label would be *couchbase_cluster:cb-example.*

The label format for the first pod is: *couchbase_node: <metadata:name>-<gen node id>*.

In the sample configuration file referenced in this topic, the label for the first pod would be *couchbase_node:cb-example-0000*.

For more information, see the Kubernetes documentation about labels.[28]

Field rules: The value of the *labels* field cannot be changed after a server has been defined.

nodeSelector

The *nodeSelector* field specifies a key-value map of the constraints on node placement for pods. For a pod to be eligible to run on a node, the node must have each of the indicated key-value pairs as labels (it can have additional labels as well). If this section is not specified, then Kubernetes will place the pod on any available node. For more information, see the Kubernetes documentation about label selectors.

Field rules: The value of the *nodeSelector* field cannot be changed after a server has been defined.

tolerations

The *tolerations* field specifies conditions upon which a node should not be selected when deploying a pod. From the sample configuration file referenced in this topic, you can see that any node with a label *app:cbapp* should not be allowed to run the pod defined in this node specification. You might do this if you have nodes dedicated for running an application using Couchbase where you don't want the database and application to be running on the same node. For more information about tolerations, see the Kubernetes documentation on taints and tolerations.[29] The tolerations section is optional.

Field rules: The value of the *tolerations* field cannot be changed after a server has been defined.

spec.servers.pod.volumeMounts

The *VolumeMounts* configuration specifies the claims to use for the storage that is used by the Couchbase Server cluster.

default

The *default* field is required when using persistent volumes. The value specifies the name of the *volumeClaimTemplate* that is used to create a persisted volume for the default path. This is always */opt/couchbase/var/lib/couchbase*. The claim must match the name of a *volumeClaimTemplate* within the spec.

data

The *data* field is the name of the *volumeClaimTemplate* that is used to create a persisted volume for the data path. When specified, the data path will be */mnt/data*. The claim must match the name of a *volumeClaimTemplate* within the spec. If this field is not specified, then a volume will not be created, and the data directory will be part of the "default" volume claim.

index

The *index* field is the name of the *volumeClaimTemplate* that is used to create a persisted volume for the index path. When specified, the index path will be */mnt/index*. The claim must match the name of a *volumeClaimTemplate* within the spec. If this field is not specified, then a volume will not be created, and the data directory will be part of the "default" volume claim.

analytics

The *analytics* field is the name of the *volumeClaimTemplate* that is used to create a persisted volume for the analytics paths. When specified, the analytics paths will be */mnt/analytics-00* (where 00 denotes the first path), with all subsequent paths having incrementing values. The claim must match the name of a *volumeClaimTemplate* within the spec. If this field is not specified, then a volume will not be created, and the data directory will be part of the "default" volume claim.

spec.volumeClaimTemplates

The *spec.volumeClaimTemplates* field defines a template of a persistent volume claim. At runtime, the Autonomous Operator will create a persistent volume from this template for each pod. Claims can request volumes from various types of storage systems as identified by the storage class name.

spec.volumeClaimTemplates.metadata

- *name* – The *metadata name* identifies the claim template. This name is used by the volumeMounts to reference which template to fulfill the mount request.

spec.volumeClaimTemplates.spec

- *storageClassName* – The *storageClassName* is required by the claim. A storageClassName provides a way for administrators to describe the classes of storage they offer. If no storageClassName is specified, then the default storage class is used. Refer to the Kubernetes documentation for more information about storage classes.[30]
- *Resources* – This defines the minimum *resources* the volume should have. Only the storage requests are valid in this context.

Deploying a Couchbase Cluster

You can create a Couchbase cluster by running one single command:

```
cbopctl create -f couchbase-cluster.yaml
```

After receiving the configuration, the Autonomous Operator automatically begins creating the cluster. The amount of time it takes to create the cluster depends on the configuration. You can track the progress of cluster creation using the *kubectl describe* command.

Here is a flow diagram (see Figure 4.5 below) that illustrates the steps described above:

- Create and run Operator.yml file
  - ○ It creates services, pods, and volumes
- Create and deploy CouchbaseCluster.yml file
  - ○ Couchbase cluster gets deployed with correct configuration, topology, persistent volumes, and server groups

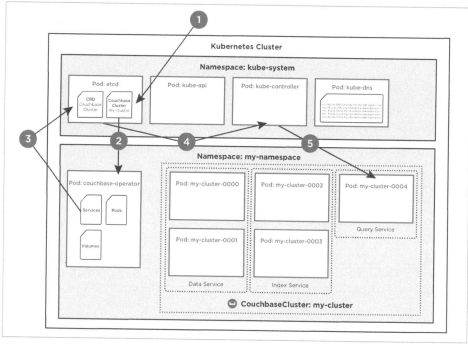

Figure 4.5: Flow diagram illustrating deployment steps

COUCHBASE AUTONOMOUS OPERATOR 1.0 HIGHLIGHTS

Automated Cluster Provisioning

Once you have defined a configuration (i.e., custom resource definition file that is like a blueprint for your Couchbase cluster), Autonomous Operator hen automatically deploys your Couchbase Server cluster based on that configuration. The Autonomous Operator takes care of all the heavy lifting, such as:

- Creating server pods
- Creating services and routes
- Creating persistent volume
- Configuring Couchbase cluster
  - Cluster settings
  - Buckets
  - Multi-dimensional scaling for Couchbase services
  - Server groups for rack/zone awareness

Once you've created a configuration file, you can use it to quickly deploy the same configuration across development, test, and production environments; or use it as a starting point to create deployments that fit even more use cases.

Read more about automated cluster provisioning.[31]

On-Demand Scalability

The scaling of a Couchbase cluster is automated through Autonomous Operator. Autonomous Operator uses the same configuration file to scale a Couchbase cluster that you used to deploy it. Scaling a Couchbase cluster up or down is as simple as updating the "size" field under "Server" configuration file, and then the Autonomous Operator autonomously handles all of the pod creation/deletion, as well as the rebalancing of nodes in and out of the Couchbase cluster.

Read more about on-demand scaling.[32]

Automated Recovery

One of the most essential aspects of a database is "data availability"; for example, in the case of node failure, how quickly data becomes available and how quickly the cluster returns to capacity.

The Autonomous Operator is always monitoring the Couchbase cluster for failures. When a node or server group failure is detected, the Autonomous Operator automatically creates a new instance either on the same host machine (preferably) or on a different host machine. It will then rebalance out the bad instances, add the new instance, and bring the cluster back up to full capacity.

If a Couchbase cluster is configured with persistent volumes, the Autonomous Operator:

1. Creates a new instance and attaches it to the same persistent volume.

2. Performs complex Couchbase operations such as delta-node recovery and warm-up operations, which reduces rebalancing data from all other instances which can be time-consuming depending on the size of data.

3. Removes the faulty instance from the Couchbase cluster and replaces it with a new instance, ensuring that the cluster is back up to the desired configuration without any loss of data.

Read more about automated recovery.[33]

High Availability Across Distributed Infrastructure

Leveraging Kubernetes labels, the Autonomous Operator is capable of automatically scheduling pod creation across failure domains and ensuring that they get added to the right Couchbase server groups for rack/zone awareness.

Combined with support for XDCR and TLS, the Autonomous Operator can automatically and securely recover a Couchbase cluster, even after the largest of physical infrastructure failures, all while remaining available to your applications.

Persistent Storage

Persistent volumes offer a way to create Couchbase pods with data that resides outside of the actual pod itself. This decoupling provides a higher degree of resilience for data within the Couchbase cluster if a node goes down or its associated pod gets terminated. Likewise, persistent volumes give you greater lexibility and efficiency in your deployment because you can let Kubernetes automatically move Couchbase pods between nodes without worrying about any downtime or data loss.

The Autonomous Operator supports some of the most popular persistent volumes from Kubernetes storage class[34] – AWS , Azure Disk, GCE , Glusterfs, Ceph RBD, and Portworx Volume.

Read more about persistent volumes.[35]

Supportability

Couchbase provides extra tools to help prevent issues from occurring in your deployment, as well as troubleshoot problems if things go wrong.

1. **Configuration validation** – Native Kubernetes tools (*kubectl* and *oc*) don't have enough knowledge about Couchbase to ensure that your cluster configuration is valid. So Couchbase developed its own command-line tool, *cbopctl*, which implements a custom subset of the *kubectl* and *oc* commands to ensure that Couchbase configurations are valid before they get uploaded to Kubernetes.

2. **Log collection** – To assist with troubleshooting and status monitoring, Couchbase developed the *cbopinfo* command-line tool to collect information and logs about any or all Couchbase clusters in a given Kubernetes namespace.

Centralized Configuration Management

The Autonomous Operator allows you to enjoy the operational benefits of Kubernetes without worrying about the administrative complexities. Instead of logging into each Couchbase cluster individually, you can manage multiple Couchbase clusters all through a single deployment of the Autonomous Operator.

5. THE FUTURE IS BRIGHT

We started this journey describing Kubernetes, how it works, and the key benefits of running your database on it. We also provided a detailed overview of Couchbase Autonomous Operator and how it makes development much easier.

At this point, you've likely started to form an opinion about Kubernetes technology and the value of running your Couchbase Server database on it.

The next step is to consider your deployment options. You have three basic choices:

1. Private clouds – Use bare metal/physical servers you own (or buy/rent) and install Open Source Kubernetes from scratch, or go with Enterprise Kubernetes from Red Hat OpenShift.

2. Public clouds – Use infrastructure from a public cloud provider and install Open Source Kubernetes from scratch or go with Enterprise Kubernetes from Red Hat OpenShift. In this case, there is a distinct advantage of not needing to buy physical hardware, but it is very different than the bare metal option.

3. Public cloud managed service – Use one of the managed offerings from the major cloud providers, for example AWS EKS, Azure AKS, and Google GKE. This route allows you fewer configuration choices but gets a lot easier than rolling out your own solution.

WHAT'S IN THE ROADMAP FOR AUTONOMOUS OPERATOR?

We shipped Couchbase Autonomous Operator 1.0 in August 2018 and, as highlighted in chapter 4, there are many great features delivered in this release. Beyond 1.0, we have aggressive plans to ship many minor versions and release 2.0 in 2019.

Features we're considering for future release:

1. Automated upgrade – Upgrade Couchbase cluster from version X to version Y, fully automated with Autonomous Operator.

2. Automated backups – Configure Couchbase cluster to run a scheduled backup on a fixed interval and leave it with Autonomous Operator to fully manage it.

3. Monitoring – Plugin to integrate with Prometheus for monitoring your Couchbase cluster.

4. Security – Define and configure your user and user roles through CouchbaseCluster configuration.

5. Usage tracking – Track Couchbase usage for self-service provisioning and usage reporting.

References

FORWARD
1. https://www.linkedin.com/in/anilkumar29/

1. WHAT IS KUBERNETES?
2. https://ai.google/research/pubs/pub43438
3. https://www.cncf.io/
4. https://www.opencontainers.org/
5. https://cloud.google.com/kubernetes-engine/docs/concepts/pod#pod_templates
6. https://kubernetes.io/docs/setup/minikube/
7. https://docs.okd.io/latest/minishift/getting-started/installing.html

2. WHY RUN COUCHBASE ON KUBERNETES?
8. https://www.cncf.io/certification/software-conformance/

3. KUBERNETES STATEFULSETS AND OPERATOR?
9. https://kubernetes.io/docs/concepts/workloads/controllers/statefulset/
10. https://kubernetes.io/docs/concepts/workloads/controllers/deployment/
11. https://kubernetes.io/docs/concepts/workloads/controllers/replicaset/
12. https://kubernetes.io/docs/concepts/storage/persistent-volumes/
13. https://bit.ly/2IQ7otQ
14. https://coreos.com/blog/introducing-operators.html
15. https://bit.ly/2C9dILC

4. INTRODUCING COUCHBASE AUTONOMOUS OPERATOR FOR KUBERNETES
16. https://bit.ly/2QIAiPc
17. https://kubernetes.io/docs/concepts/services-networking/service/
18. https://docs.couchbase.com/operator/1.0/prerequisite-and-setup.html
19. https://docs.couchbase.com/operator/1.0/best-practices.html
20. https://www.couchbase.com/downloads?family=kubernetes
21. https://hub.docker.com/r/couchbase/operator/
22. https://docs.couchbase.com/operator/1.0/demo.html
23. https://docs.couchbase.com/operator/1.0/tls.html
24. https://kubernetes.io/docs/concepts/configuration/secret/
25. https://bit.ly/2IQAtp6
26. https://docs.couchbase.com/operator/1.0/scaling-couchbase.html
27. https://bit.ly/2RG0kUF
28. https://bit.ly/2EdbkGl
29. https://bit.ly/2N1UgY3
30. https://kubernetes.io/docs/concepts/storage/storage-classes/
31. https://docs.couchbase.com/operator/1.0/deploying-couchbase.html
32. https://docs.couchbase.com/operator/1.0/scaling-couchbase.html
33. https://docs.couchbase.com/operator/1.0/node-recovery.html
34. https://kubernetes.io/docs/concepts/storage/storage-classes/#provisioner
35. https://docs.couchbase.com/operator/1.0/persisted-volumes-guide.html